Original title:
Woman to Woman

Author: Swan Charm
Editor: Jessica Elisabeth Luik
ISBN 978-9916-39-151-8

Woman to Woman

Swan Charm

Pearls of Her Path

Along the cobbled streets she walks,
Her silent dreams like whispered talks,
Every step a precious stone,
A memory in time alone.

The morning mist, her serene face,
Each pearl of dew, her path does trace,
In every one, her laughter's caught,
A gallery of battles fought.

Sunlight threads through trees above,
Casting shadows on the truths she wove,
Those pearls shine with tales untold,
In her story, they're pure gold.

Maiden Voyage Tales

Upon the seas, so vast and wide,
A young sail's shadow by the tide,
The maiden voyage calls her name,
Each wave, a page of newfound fame.

The hull embraces briny deep,
While stars their ancient secrets keep,
Tales of yore and whispered lore,
The ocean's heart begins to roar.

With compass true and sextant keen,
She navigates through scenes unseen,
Exploring lands where myths prevail,
Her story's wake leaves a bold trail.

Goddesses in Discourse

In the hall of whispering divines,
The goddesses weave their fate's designs,
The discourse flows like ancient wine,
Words as rich as a golden mine.

Athena's wit, sharp and precise,
Artemis speaks of moonlit heist,
Aphrodite's beauty, ever pure,
Demeter's bounty, nature's allure.

Past marble columns their voices soar,
Power and grace forevermore,
In debate, they mold the world's course,
With conviction, they fuel its force.

Lullabies for Ladies

Lullabies spin through the night's embrace,
For the ladies draped in moon's soft lace,
Whispered gently to end the day,
Guiding dreams along their way.

Stars twinkle as a gentle hush,
Over cheeks flushed with a rosy blush,
Cradled in the Milky Way's arms,
Guarded from all earthly harms.

The serene song of the nightingale,
Weaves through the slumberous, quiet vale,
Singing peace until morning's light,
Cocooned in dreams throughout the night.

A Tapestry of Timeless Ties

Within the loom of years entwined,
Each thread a tale of kin so dear,
A fabric wrought with love designed,
Time's handiwork, both far and near.

A weave of joy, a patterned plight,
Colors dance in harmony,
Generations in each stitch tight,
Pledging endless symphony.

The seams of sorrows held within,
Mend the heartaches of the past,
Silken memories begin,
A tapestry to forever last.

In every fiber, life's embrace,
A story bound in each tight twist,
Our lineage within the lace,
A legacy that will persist.

Maidens' Mirth

By the brook the maidens played,
Laughter echoed through the glade,
Footsteps light on the soft earth,
Hearts abloom with untold mirth.

Crown of flowers, golden hair,
Gaiety filling the fresh air,
Sunshine smiles, secrets share,
Youthful joys without a care.

Dances twirl in the meadow's arms,
All nature charmed by youthful charms,
Ribbons fly, sweet and free,
Amidst a world of fantasy.

As twilight folds its gentle wings,
Their laughter in the ether rings,
In the hush of evening's birth,
Remains the echo of maidens' mirth.

The Graces' Gavotte

Gracefully they take the stage,
A timeless dance, the world's their page,
In harmony they move and weave,
To the Gavotte, the Graces cleave.

Each step inscribes the air with ease,
Their gestures stir a gentle breeze,
As though the heavens do applaud,
The beauty of the gods, unflawed.

A trio twirls, in pure delight,
Their gowns aglow with starry light,
Poise and beauty here alight,
The dance endures into the night.

With every beat, their grace endures,
The melody of cosmos lures,
In choreography divine,
The Graces' Gavotte, eternally enshrined.

Ribbons of Her Reminiscence

Wistful eyes gaze upon the years,
As memories unravel, fears,
Ribbons winding through her past,
Each a moment meant to last.

A tapestry she weaves in mind,
With strands of laughter, tears entwined,
Silken threads of bygone days,
In the heart's loom, nostalgia plays.

Sunset hues her thoughts adorn,
Golden moments, love was born,
Ribbons twist, a dance of fate,
In life's parade, they resonate.

Through time these ribbons gently sway,
A life's story in array,
Each a chapter, neatly penned,
In her reminiscence, without end.

Steel Magnolia Sonnets

Beneath the southern sun, blooms tough and fair,
Steel magnolias withstand the hardest air.
Their petals soft, but roots grip deep and strong,
In adversity, they find their sweetest song.

Through storms they stand, a gentle, fierce array,
Each branch a testament to night and day.
Resilient hearts, with beauty sharp and keen,
In each unfold, life’s myriad scenes are seen.

With grace they weather life’s relentless gale,
Their fragrance a soft, enduring tale.
Unyielding yet with tenderness they sway,
Like steel magnolias, we learn and stay.

Kindred Spirits' Canticles

Upon the path where kindred spirits tread,
Shared dreams take flight, by same bright fancy led.
Whispers of joy, like leaves in playful dance,
Encircle souls in serendipitous chance.

Through life's vast realm of wonder, side by side,
With spirits woven, in trust we confide.
Our voices harmonize in life's grand choir,
Each note a spark, together they inspire.

In kindred bonds, we find our hearts' refrain,
Echoing each other through joy and pain.
Ever entwined, our fates both intertwine,
In canticles of kinship, we align.

Ancestral Apron Strings

In woven threads of history's embrace,
We wear the aprons of our kinfolk's grace.
Stains of toil, love's labor softly penned,
On fabrics time and memories transcend.

Each knot and fold, a legend to unfold,
Stories of hearth and kin are gently told.
The fabric holds, through times of feast or famine,
Apron strings, like roots, give life its gamut.

Generations past, hands both rough and deft,
Within their craft, a lasting legacy left.
Bound by blood and thread, through time we sing,
The hymns of love from ancestral apron strings.

Queens in Conversation

In realms of thought, where mighty queens converse,
Each word a jewel, their wisdom to disperse.
Crowned with insight that time alone refines,
In dialogue, the essence of power shines.

Ideas as scepters, raised in regal poise,
They speak of realms that force cannot destroy.
In symphony, their discourse weaves a bond,
A noble gathering across the beyond.

Through eons, their enduring voices reign,
In counsel, they explore life's vast domain.
With each exchange, their majesty preserves,
A lineage of queens, through words conserved.

In the Garden of Gaia

Beneath the ancient boughs we tread,
Along the paths where dewdrops wed,
Gaia's breath whispers through the leaves,
In her embrace, our spirit heaves.

Her colors blend in wildflower seas,
With fragrant air, the zephyrs breeze,
Earth's heartbeat underfoot, so mild,
In this garden, we're nature's child.

Verdant life in endless bloom,
Where butterflies in sunlight zoom,
In Gaia's garden, we find peace,
Her tender cradle, our release.

Conversations Over Cosmos

Stellar whispers cross the void,
Hushed murmurs that cannot be toyed,
In the ink of space, words deploy,
Cosmic tales of sorrow and joy.

Galactic symphonies unfold,
In nebulous stories, eons told,
Silent dialogues, brave and bold,
In the vast, our thoughts we mold.

Orbital dances weave our speech,
Each planet with a lesson to teach,
Over cosmos, our voices reach,
In starlight, we beseech.

Legacy of the Lotus

Rooted in mire, unstained it blooms,
A lotus legacy in watery tombs,
Purest white in murky glooms,
Defying silt, its beauty looms.

In petals lie the silent tales,
Of strength that through the mud prevails,
Life's trials that a heart assails,
Yet in this bloom, peace inhales.

It rises with a tranquil grace,
A soulful journey from its base,
A legacy carved in time and space,
In the lotus, life we embrace.

The Dance of the Divine

The cosmos twirls in divine reel,
Stars and planets set to keel,
Through the dark, a waltz they feel,
In celestial dance, they heal.

With every spin, a purpose found,
Infinite spirals tightly wound,
Galactic rhythms tightly bound,
In the dance, we are astound.

Black holes pirouette in might,
Comets streak with tails alight,
In the divine dance, take flight,
A cosmic spectacle, pure and bright.

The Amazons' Anthem

In whispers of the ancient trees, we stand
With hearts aflame and power in our hands
Our echoes stir the spirits of the land
United, fierce, as Amazons we band

Boldly we ride where shadows weave and wind
Through moonlit paths, our destinies aligned
In sisterhood, our courage intertwined
No foe nor fear can ever break our mind

Our arrows soar like eagles on the breeze
Our swords strike true, our legacy to seize
In harmony with Earth's unyielding tease
We live, we love, the Amazon decrees

So hear our anthem rise to skies above
A chant of strength, of freedom, and of love

Opus of the Orchid

In silent grace, the orchid blooms alone
Its beauty speaks in hues yet to be known
A soft sonata to the wild it's shown
Through every petal, nature’s art is sown

A symphony of colors rich and pure
A testament to elegance demure
In tranquil poise, it dances, so mature
An opus of the earth, untouched and sure

With roots sunk deep where secret waters flow
It gathers life from mystical below
In undisturbed serenity it grows
Reflecting rays of the sun’s gentle glow

Beneath the forest’s green and grand arcade
The orchid’s opus quietly displayed

The Queen's Quill

Beneath the crown, a mind of boundless thought
Each word a gem, from deepest wisdom brought
The Queen’s quill dances, battlefields are fought
On parchment plains where silent wars are wrought

In ink, she spills her realm's majestic dreams
Her quill conducts the realm's poetic streams
Through every stroke, a greater purpose gleams
Uniting all within her regal themes

She scripts the tales of old and days to come
The heart of kingdoms beating like a drum
Her vision shapes an empire, then some
With every line, a legacy’s outcome

The Queen’s quill, a scepter of her reign
A power wielded, forged by intellect's train

Croon of the Camellias

Adorned in velvet red, blooms softly sing
The camellia's tune starts with spring
Their petals croon, a luscious murmuring
In garden’s choir, quiet harmony they bring

Their scent weaves through the air, a subtle call
With every note, they hold the winter’s thrall
In beauty’s court, they stand both proud and tall
A gentle power vested in their sprawl

They whisper secrets with a floral tone
A language known to nature’s ear alone
Their song of growth, where peace and calm are sown
In nature’s croon, a soothing undertone

Behold the camellias in their prime
Their silent melody, timeless, sublime

The Oracle’s Offering

In the temple's heart, the silence reigns,
With ancient whispers of the uttering stone.
Futures foretold in the flickering flames,
Destinies read where the omens are shown.

Veiled in mystery, she speaks in dreams,
The Oracle's voice, both cryptic and clear.
Guiding the seekers to bind their seams,
Offering truths that the brave wish to hear.

In her eyes, the cosmos dance and swirl,
Time’s tapestry woven with delicate hands.
Her prophecies unfurl, the future to curl,
A map of the stars, in shifting sands.

She stands alone with the fates aligned,
An offering of hope for those entwined.

Whispers Across the Willow

Gentle breezes murmur low,
Lifting the willow’s emerald bough.
Whispers soft and secrets shared,
Nature’s quiet message bared.

The willow weeps in serene grace,
Leaves caress the water's face.
Each ripple tells a tale of old,
Of love and loss that the waters hold.

Sunset's fire in the sky does glow,
Heeding the whispers that the willows know.
Twilight's hush, and the world's soft sigh,
Underneath the vast, ink-black sky.

These whispers stretch through time and space,
A subtle presence in the willow’s embrace,
Carrying words where the heart flows,
In the gentle dance of the weeping boughs.

Enchantresses' Elegy

By pale moonlight, they weaved their song,
A harmony of power where they belong.
Beneath the stars, their circle drawn,
Night's enchantresses till the dawn.

Their chanting rises, soft and strong,
An elegy for what's gone wrong.
With every note, they right a wrong,
Ancient words they've known so long.

The magic thrums within their hold,
A tapestry of mystic fold.
Through silver threads of fate remold,
The enchantresses' tale is told.

In the hush of night, their voices fade,
Leaving behind the spells they've made.
As dawn alights on the forest's glade,
The enchantresses rest in the shadowy shade.

Serenade for the Sovereigns

Lutes and lyres for the king and queen,
Their reign as fair as any ever seen.
The minstrels play, the people lean,
To hear the serenade for the sovereign's sheen.

The melody caresses like a soft velvet glove,
A token of loyalty, of deep, boundless love.
Each note a crown woven from above,
A musical embrace as gentle as a dove.

The sovereigns listen from their thrones so grand,
To the serenade that flows through the land.
The harmony echoes at their command,
A tribute to the rulers of this noble strand.

As twilight descends and the stars start to sing,
The serenade fades like the passing of spring.
In the hearts of the subjects, hope does it bring,
For the sovereigns' grace under heaven's wing.

Seamstresses of the Sky

In twilight's loom they gather thread,
To weave the night with stars so bright.
Silken needles dip and ply,
Stitching dreams into the quiet sky.

With fingers deft as zephyrs sigh,
The moonlit maids embroider high.
Each star a sequin, slyly placed,
In the tapestry of the cosmic space.

Their gowns of nebulae unfurled,
Across the canvas of the world.
In constellation patterns, they confide,
The secrets that the heavens hide.

By first light's break, their work unseen,
Leaves behind a sky serene.
The sun ascends, their stitches stay,
Till dusk returns, and they resume their ballet.

Memories of Muses

Muses dwelled in memories old,
In ancient tales, in whispers told.
The spark of art they did bestow,
In every heart a vibrant glow.

Their voices like a summer breeze,
That danced through attic's dusty eaves.
In every note a story lies,
A painting's hue, a poet's sighs.

In dreams at night, they come to dance,
Igniting sleepy minds by chance.
With inspiration's sacred flame,
To sculpt our thoughts and give them frame.

Now in the quiet of the mind,
The muses' echoes we still find.
In undying legacy they thrive,
Within our hearts, they're still alive.

The Oracle's Ode

Oh Oracle, in shadowed shrine,
Speaks in riddles, speaks in rhymes.
Futures told in smoky haze,
Paths revealed through mystic maze.

Eyes that see through veils of time,
Witness truth in every chime.
Ancient words in silence spun,
Unveiling what will be done.

Chanting prophecies of old,
With visions clear and futures bold.
Embracing fate with every breath,
Transcending life, transcending death.

Attend the whispers that entwine,
In every omen, in every sign.
The oracle's wisdom, forever a guide,
In cryptic verses, the truths they hide.

Timeless Tresses

A cascade of timeless tresses falls,
O'er shoulders like the ancient walls.
Each strand, a history unfurls,
In the dance of the wind, it twirls.

Ageless locks, in sunlight spun,
In every fiber, stories run.
From maiden's blush to crone's gray hue,
A lifetime's diary, a spectrum true.

In each curl's coil, the hours keep,
From waking dawn to restful sleep.
In braids and buns, the moments nest,
A chronicle of life expressed.

Hair, a crown of wisdom earned,
Through years of lessons, gently learned.
Though time may pass and fashions shift,
The timeless tresses are nature's gift.

Velvet Voices

Whispers weave through the waning light,
In velvet tones of the passing night,
Each word a thread in the dark's embrace,
Sewing shadows with silken grace.

Echoes dance in a soft refrain,
Through the hush of the slumbering plain,
Speaks the breeze with a gentle power,
In the quiet of the midnight hour.

Serenade of the stars above,
Crooning tales of forgotten love,
Velvet voices, tender and true,
Humming hymns of the night's deep blue.

Crescendoing in the dreamer's mind,
Where secrets of the heart unwind,
In tender tunes, the night imparts,
A symphony of tranquil hearts.

Bridal Bloom Ballads

In gowns of white, they float on air,
With blossoms braided through their hair,
Bridal blooms in ballads sung,
Each petal's praise, from joy is wrung.

Aisles adorned with floral grace,
Behold love in its purest face,
Petals echo the march divine,
For two hearts in ballad entwined.

Whispered vows 'neath arches tall,
Where roses climb and lilies call,
The bridal ballad softly sways,
In the hallowed hush of wedding days.

The bouquet's thrown, a hopeful creed,
For new love’s bloom, from this seed,
A melody in petals cast,
Bridal bloom ballads, timeless, vast.

Mistresses of Memory

They dwell in halls of bygone days,
In the silence where the past replays,
Mistresses of memory sing,
With voices that make the rafters ring.

Each echo holds a time long gone,
A laughter's peal, a dusk, a dawn,
In their hands, the past revives,
On the loom where history thrives.

They spin the yarns of yesteryears,
Tinged with joy and salted tears,
A chronicle of love and strife,
Weaving the tapestry of life.

Forgotten not, the tales they keep,
In the archives of the deep,
Mistresses with time's keys kept,
Guard the moments that we've wept.

Silken Sister Secrets

In the hush of hidden rooms,
Silken whispers, sister blooms,
Secrets sewn in sisterhood's seam,
Shimmer in the moon's soft beam.

Giggles wrapped in mystery's guise,
Locked within each other's eyes,
Pledges made where shadows play,
Secrets sisters never betray.

Threads of trust in friendship woven,
Sisterhood's unspoken token,
Silken ties that will not part,
Secrets safe within the heart.

In the quiet of sister's bower,
Shared are dreams of gentle power,
Beneath the stars that secrets hear,
Silken sisters hold them dear.

Harmonies of Hera

In gardens where the peacocks roam, beneath the sky's wide dome,
Two hearts entwined in ancient grace, where love has found its home.
Majestic as the queen of gods, their whispers softly plea,
Harmonious, the chorus soars, an ageless melody.

Upon a throne of olive leaves, where wisdom's roots run deep,
Golden apples glisten bright, within their sacred keep.
Each note a vow, each chord a bond, in Hera's watchful eyes,
Hymns of loyalty ascend, wrapping hearts in ties.

Heiresses of the Hearth

In the twilight's ember glow, where hearth fires burn and fade,
Daughters of the ancient flame, protect what time has made.
Their whispered chants weave through the smoke, like thread through weaver's loom,
Guardians of the glowing coals, defy the darkened gloom.

With hands that shape the destiny, of every fleeting spark,
They feed the flames that warm the soul, pushing back the dark.
Ancestral torch passed hand to hand, from age to storied age,
The heiresses of hearthside tales, scribe wisdom on life's page.

Conversations by Candlelight

Two shadows dance to candlelight, where secrets softly bloom,
Spilling tales like molten wax, in the privacy of gloom.
A flicker whispers truths untold, in the stillness of the night,
Conversations thread their way, until the dawn's first light.

With words that spill like silver streams, and thoughts that curve and bend,
To candle's flame they bare their souls, where darkness is a friend.
In the quiet exchange of heartfelt chimes, they find their rare reprieve,
Till candles weep their last goodbye, and night takes its leave.

The Sheroes' Stanza

In pages of the silent past, where sheroes' deeds are sung,
Valiant tales of daring quests, from worried hearts are wrung.
Their armor shines with courage, their spirits ever fierce,
With every stanza that's inscribed, their legacies pierce.

They wield their words as weapons sharp, and shields of solid verse,
Defeating dragons of despair, curses they reverse.
In every line a battle won, a triumph over fear,
The sheroes' stanza rings out loud, for all willing to hear.

Feminine Flourishes

Gentle curves in the river's flow,
A touch so soft, a warm, faint glow.
Nature whispers in tender verse,
The strength of womanhood, diverse.

Beneath the moon, a silent plea,
Grace in the night, so wild and free.
Stars reflect in the calm, deep sea,
Endless beauty, strong and carefree.

The blooming fields of luscious life,
Beyond the roles of mother, wife.
Petals unfold without a fuss,
Within each woman’s heart, a lotus.

In every laugh, a melody,
In every tear, a sea of empathy.
Lives intertwined in tapestry,
Feminine essence, forever free.

Heroines' Hymns

Masked not in capes, but courage true,
Across the ages, they've marched through.
Bearing torches in darkest nights,
Brave heroines in endless fights.

On battlegrounds of bias and scorn,
They've risen early, they've weathered storms.
Their anthems loud, their spirits worn,
Yet in their eyes, the new dawn forms.

Through the silence of history's pages,
Their voices roar from hidden stages.
Defying the limits, setting trends,
Heroines whose bravery never ends.

Charging forth, no chain can bind,
The power of an unconquered mind.
Their hymns of victory, sung so bold,
In their fearless hearts, the future's told.

Matriarchs' Muse

Wisdom etched in every line,
Countenance serene, divine.
Matriarchs from times of yore,
Kindred spirits we adore.

Weaving tales by fireside’s light,
Guiding through the coldest night.
Generations in their gaze,
In their love, a guiding blaze.

Strong as pillars forged in time,
Yet in their touch, a peace sublime.
Sacrifice their silent hymn,
In their wake, we follow them.

Ancestral whispers in the breeze,
Their legacy will never cease.
Through us flows their timeless muse,
In our veins, their strength infused.

Yin Reflections

Quiet waters, deep and still,
The Yin within, a tranquil quill.
Reflecting moons on silver lakes,
In stillness, the soul awakes.

Harmony in ebb and flow,
In every leaf, life’s gentle glow.
The Yin’s soft shadow, cool embrace,
A nurturing force, a tender grace.

Balancing the sun's bold fire,
The quiet whispers of desire.
In Yin’s reflection, find our part,
The silent beat of nature’s heart.

Embrace the night, the cool, dark earth,
Yin's quiet power, giving birth.
In the balance, life unfolds,
Within the Yin, the truth it holds.

Nectar of the Nymphs

In a glade where the wild thyme blows,
Under the gaze of the endless skies,
The nectar as pure as morning glows,
A secret potion the forest belies.

Amidst the emerald leaves it lies afar,
Glistening droplets on petals array,
Nectar of nymphs, in a dewdrop's star,
Coveted elixir, where sprites do play.

Floral whispers in the tranquil air,
Its taste is lore, from an ancient hymn,
Sipping the essence of life so rare,
Eternal youth at the vessel's brim.

Dancing light through a canopy laced,
Nature's ambrosia, subtly embraced.

Rhapsody of the Roses

Velvet red beneath the crescent moon's glow,
Guardians of the garden's secret tune,
Each thorn a note in the night's shadow,
Singing of love's sweet, fragrant boon.

Petals unfolding in tender embrace,
Whispering ballads to the stars above,
In every bloom, a heart's tender grace,
Painting the air with scents of love.

Thickets of roses in harmonious spree,
A symphony of hues in the evening air,
Romancing the breeze, swaying carefree,
In the rhapsody of nature's affair.

Crimson, peach, white entwine in dance,
A floral melody, in perpetual romance.

The Chalice and the Charm

In the hall where the shadows play,
A chalice wrought from silver dreams,
In its depths, the starlight's sway,
The charm of ages in its seams.

Mysteries held in a vessel pure,
Carved runes upon its ancient side,
Whispers of a potion to allure,
Where magic and the divine reside.

Drink with care from the ornate cup,
For within its hold, a power dwells,
The charm, it stirs, to raise or disrupt,
Imbued with enchantments and spells.

Reflecting the fates in liquid's sheen,
Where destiny's touch and myth convene.

Maiden's Melancholy

In her eyes, a wistful shimmering lake,
Where dreams once danced, now quiet lies,
The sigh of the heart when it aches,
Echoes softly as she whispers her goodbyes.

Through halls of memory, she treads alone,
Clad in sorrows of a silken shroud,
Each step a verse of a lonesome song,
Sung to the moon behind a cloud.

Yet in her gaze, a flickering light,
A spark that yearns for breaking dawn,
The will to chase away the night,
Wherein her silent strength is drawn.

Maiden's melancholy, bittersweet and deep,
In the tapestry of life, a thread to keep.

Sisterhood Symphony

United by bonds unseen, a thread of grace unfurled,
Within their laughter resonance, a melody is twirled.
In every shared secret, a symphony's soft sigh,
Sisters in arms weave the tapestry of the sky.

Parallel pulses in harmony, like the notes of a song,
Navigating life’s steep cliffs, they make each other strong.
The cadence of support, where joy and sorrow blend,
Sisters compose the music that never has an end.

Their whispers in the moonlight, a chorus of serenity,
They dance through life’s crescendos and its tender lenity.
In unison, their dreams lift, on wings of silent trust,
A sisterhood symphony, thriving bold and just.

Maternal Echoes

Whispers of the past that hum through time and space,
Echoes of maternal love, a never-fading grace.
In every nurturing touch, history is retold,
The warmth of a mother's embrace, a bond that will never fold.

The lessons of lifetimes, carried in her voice,
A cascade of wisdom, giving her child a choice.
Through patience and sacrifice, her legacy takes flight,
Maternal echoes guiding through the day and night.

A laugh that dissipates the shadows, a comfort in the storm,
Her strength, a lighthouse beacon, consistently performing.
The tapestry she weaves with time's delicate threads,
Are the maternal echoes, where all love's path leads.

Daughters of the Same Stars

Born from cosmic dust, beneath heaven's grand arch,
Daughters of the same stars, on their luminous march.
Illuminated by moonlight and kissed by the sun,
Sharing the same spark since life has begun.

Each dream a constellation, drawn in their eyes,
Crafting their destinies under the same skies.
Stardust in their veins, galaxies in their heart,
Navigating their journeys, though eons apart.

Mirror of the firmament, in each soul is found,
A fragment of the cosmos, to which they are bound.
Daughters of starlight, with hopes that flare and dance,
United under the tapestry of cosmic expanse.

Her Whispered Strength

In the hush of early dawn, her whispered strength begins,
A silent fortitude that stirs as each new day spins.
She speaks in actions tender, in the courage of her stance,
In the quiet determination of her unwavering glance.

A soft and steady murmuring, like the wind through ancient trees,
Her whispered strength reverberates, setting captive spirits free.
A testament to endurance, to the will that won't relent,
In every word not spoken, in every message sent.

In the warmth of her laughter, in the solace of her sigh,
Lies the power of a whisper that never dares to die.
With every trial she faces, with love that stands the length,
There lies her greatest power, in her whispered strength.

Ladies of the Lake Revisited

Beneath the shroud of morning mist,
Aloof, where water lilies kissed,
The ladies dance, their fate be-twined,
In whispered legends, lost in time.

They hold the secrets none can speak,
With silken robes and cheeks so meek,
Upon the glassy lake they glide,
Their silent ripples far and wide.

In moonlit grace, they softly tread,
A watery realm, their silent bed,
Where knights and poets long to drink,
The wisdom deep beneath the brink.

Each lady of the lake, so fair,
Entrusts the keeper's solemn care,
Of stories old and magic spun,
Till stars do fade and rise the sun.

Cradle Song Silhouettes

Moonbeams cast on nursery walls,
Silhouettes of cradles fall,
Rocking gently through the night,
Bathing babes in silver light.

Hush of night-time's lulling song,
Cooing soft, where dreams belong,
Infant eyes in slumber's hold,
Tales of warmth, in whispers told.

Stars peek in with twinkling eyes,
Casting wishes from the skies,
As a cradle's song takes flight,
In the theater of the night.

Rest, my baby, fret no more,
In the silhouette-filled lore,
May this cradle song endear,
Moments sweet and memories clear.

Grandmother's Garden Secrets

Grandmother's garden, rows meticulously kept,
Laden with the secrets that the earthbound whispers wept,
Each bloom a chapter of her life's unfolding tale,
In petal-scripts and colors, through time remain they hale.

The roses speak of love's sweet kiss, the thorns of sorrow's sting,
Sunflowers, heavy with the gaze where memories cling,
The violets shy and hidden 'midst the greenery's embrace,
Embodiments of secrets in this tranquil resting place.

Fragrant herbs amidst the blooms, their scents the air conspire,
To tell of healing hands and hearts that came before the pyre,
The garden path, a labyrinth where secrets safely wind,
In grandmother's horticulture, history entwined.

With every seed and sapling laid, with tender care and art,
The garden secrets flourished from grandmother's gentle heart,
She tended not just soil, but souls with every nurturing deed,
Within her garden's secrets, life's essence is the seed.

Femininity in Verse

In every gentle verse, a form of strength we find,
A soft resilience in the folds of femininity defined,
From whispered fears to roaring seas, a range so vast and wide,
The essence of a woman's heart, with every pulse inside.

She writes in verse her silent thoughts, her hopes, her dreams, her pain,
The poetry a canvas for her soul's enduring reign,
Through stanzas steeped with tenderness, her spirit takes to flight,
In metaphors and similes, her story finds the light.

Her verse it weaves from silken threads of joy and deep despair,
A tapestry of life itself, love's pattern etched with care,
The cadence of her presence in the rhythm of the lines,
Femininity in verse that through the ages shines.

The quills may change, the ink may fade, but ever does she write,
The narrative of womanhood, in shadows or in light,
For every poem bears her touch, a testament, a part,
The beat that echoes softly is the drumming of her heart.

The Carousel of Clio

Upon the carousel of time, Clio spins,
With every turn, a new age begins.
History's horses, up and down they roam,
Echoes of the past in the silence shown.

Gilded steeds with manes of flowing lore,
Tales of triumph, struggle, peace, and war.
Round and round the muse of history rides,
Moments captured where her grace abides.

Enchanted by her gentle, steady whirl,
Past and present in her dance unfurl.
The carousel of Clio knows no end,
For in each revolution, narratives blend.

Embrace the ride, with eyes and heart wide,
In the turning cycles, wisdom shall confide.
Her carousel spins, a tale anew,
Each horse, a chapter, a world to view.

Epochs of Eve

Eve, the mother of all epochs, stands tall,
Through her eyes, we've witnessed empires fall.
In each phase, a whisper of her might,
Generations blossom in her eternal light.

From Eden's gates to the cities of man,
Each age an epoch in her vast plan.
A lineage carved from her tender hand,
As seasons turn at her silent command.

She governs eras with a soft caress,
Cradling civilizations in periods of progress.
In her gaze, the sands of time flow,
Bearing legacies only she can bestow.

Eve walks through centuries with grace,
Her footprints, the progress we embrace.
In her essence, the epochs we weave,
Each strand of history, an Epoch of Eve.

Confetti of Cronies

In the halls of laughter and luminescent nights,
Confetti of cronies, a sprinkling of delights.
Boisterous banter fills the air so thick,
Friendship's fabric, woven strong and quick.

Shared secrets and jokes only we know,
Through times of high tide and undertow.
Moments fluttering down like colored rain,
Memories that will forever remain.

In our circle, every quip a treasure,
Each word weighed in units of pleasure.
Laughter dances in our ring so tight,
Illumined by joy, all hearts ignite.

Confetti of cronies, oh how it flies,
Scattering moments 'neath the jovial skies.
True friendship, an unbreakable dance,
In the confetti's flight, our spirits prance.

The Veil's Venture

Beyond the veil, where mysteries enshroud,
Adventures whispered, in echoes aloud.
Each step taken a venture anew,
Unseen paths bathed in ethereal hue.

The veil's venture, a journey so rare,
Shadows dance with a secretive flair.
Within the folds, where veiled truths lie,
Silent wonders subtly pass by.

Unknown realms just beyond the sight,
Waiting for the brave to embrace the night.
The veil parts ways for the heart sincere,
Revealing worlds that once seemed so sheer.

Step through the veil, let your spirit soar,
Discover realms untouched, folklore.
Embrace the unknown, with a fearless heart,
In the veil's venture, be ready to start.

Chanson for the Charmed

Beneath the willow's whispering shade,
Where secrets in the dappled glade,
Charmed melodies softly flow,
In rhythms only hearts can decode.

Within the zephyr's gentle sigh,
The leaves perform a lullaby,
Swaying in a tender trance,
In the meadow's emerald expanse.

Eyes alight with moonbeam's kiss,
Dreamers yearn for midnight's bliss,
The charm's alive with magic spun,
By threads of silver, quietly done.

Stars above in quiet mirth,
Celebrate the charm's rebirth,
Whispering winds carry the tune,
Hummed by the cradle of the moon.

The Chalice Chant

In the hall of echoing splendor,
Where the chalice guards the dreams,
Silver whispers of defender,
Flow like softly murmured streams.

Echoes of ancient stories,
Fill the chalice to the brim,
Glowing with its inner glories,
Chanting an immortal hymn.

Round the ring of gathered kinfolk,
Tales are drunk in hearty sips,
Binding ties that never broke,
Past the cloak of an eclipse.

Threads of fate weave through the night,
As the chant grows deep and wide,
In the chalice, truth takes flight,
On history's relentless tide.

Echoes of Empresses

Through the corridors of time,
Whispers float of power sublime,
Echoes of empresses, regal and grand,
Who once ruled with a steady hand.

Their voices soft as silk unspun,
Commanding the rise and set of sun,
Each echo a wave from the past's vast sea,
Resounding with solemnity.

In palaces adorned with gold,
Their stories in hushed tones are told,
Of empresses draped in authority’s grace,
Time's tapestry they boldly encase.

These echoes resound in history's hall,
As crowns and thrones eventually fall,
Yet their legacy forever impresses,
In the echoes of ancient empresses.

Sapphire Sisterhood

Sisters of the sapphire night,
United under starry light,
With bonds as deep as the ocean’s hue,
Their allegiance forever true.

Clasped hands cast a circle wide,
Where secrets and dreams coincide,
Each star a vow of sisterhood’s creed,
A pact that time cannot impede.

In the quiet glow of the moon’s embrace,
Sapphire sisters share their grace,
Their whispers weave through the dark expanse,
In unity's mesmerizing dance.

Though dawn may part their tender midst,
The sisterhood in twilight persists,
For in the night’s most precious gem,
Their kindred spirits convene again.

Brocade and Bravery

In silken tapestries of lore,
Where threadbare tales of battle soar,
Each stitch a saga, hemmed in glory,
Brocade binds the brave man's story.

Crafted on the loom of time,
Bravery's pattern, bold, sublime,
Golden yarns in valor's weave,
Heroes in their legends leave.

A tapestry so rich, so vast,
Embroidered with deeds of the past,
Velvet valor, courage spun,
Bravery's cloth, never undone.

Heroes' hues in every fold,
Tales of valor, brightly told,
The brocade of the brave remains,
Preserving their noble strains.

Mothers of the Moonlight

Beneath the soft and silver glow,
Mothers' whispers, hushed and low,
Guiding through the night so bright,
In the tender arms of lunar light.

Their words like cradle songs at night,
In moonbeam robes of purest white,
Calm the fears that children hold,
With love more precious than of gold.

Gentle keepers of the night,
In celestial dance, they take their flight,
Each a guardian, a silent grace,
With tender mercy filling space.

Mothers of the moonlight, shine,
With love that's known to transcend time,
The nurturing glow upon each face,
In their care, our hearts embrace.

Ebony Enigmas

Shadows cloak the midnight sphere,
Whispers of enigmas near,
Ebony secrets, kept untold,
Puzzles in the dark unfold.

Mysteries wrapped in velvet night,
Sable riddles dodging light,
In dusk's embrace, they quietly stay,
Holding dawn's reveal at bay.

Cryptic keeps of unseen things,
Behind the night, where wonder clings,
Each enigmatic, ebony guise,
Hides a truth beneath the skies.

Darkness holds its wise enigmas,
Cloaked in night's black panoramas,
Seek the secrets skillfully hid,
In ebony's puzzle, the truth amid.

Unveiling the Elysian

A realm unseen, a land of peace,
Where all the toils of life shall cease,
The elusive quest for the divine,
In the Elysian, we entwine.

Fields of grace to wander, free,
From earthly bonds, souls flee,
To unveil the mystic Elysian dream,
Beyond where mortal eyes have been.

A paradise penned in poets' lore,
With gossamer gates on tranquil shore,
Visions of splendor, pure, unspoken,
The shroud of mystery gently broken.

In the haze of legend's light,
The Elysian fields bloom into sight,
Revelations of the seraphic plane,
In the unveiling, bliss remains.

The Crimson Bond

In twilight's gentle sigh, our hearts do speak,
A crimson bond, not frail, a bond not weak.
Through threads of fate, our souls are interlaced,
In love's warm grip, our union is embraced.

A common pulse through veins of time does run,
Two spirits dance, eclipsing setting sun.
In life's grand waltz, we sway with trust and care,
Our bond, a fortress built on something rare.

Through stormy trials, a steadfast ship we steer,
Our bond, the anchor through each passing year.
United strength in every test, we find,
A red-hued link, by destiny designed.

In whispered dreams, where secrets are confessed,
Our bond's bright flame within our chest is blessed.
Harmonious, our song forever calls,
A crimson bond, unbroken by life's squalls.

Motherhood Murmurs

In quiet hours before dawn's first light,
Motherhood murmurs through the calm of night.
Soft lullabies escape in tender tune,
A dance of stars beneath the waning moon.

To soothe the cries that break the still of air,
With gentle touch and whispers like a prayer.
Each tear wiped away, each shiver calmed,
In mother’s arms, the world retreats, embalmed.

The sun arises, chores in tow will surge,
Yet, steadfast love in every act will merge.
She wields the day’s demands with quiet grace,
Her murmured hopes a soothing, tranquil space.

Through every phase, her vigil never ends,
Her murmured wisdom, life’s soft amends.
In every trial, a mother’s murmurs soar,
A steadfast ship to guide us to the shore.

Sisterly Shadows

In light and dark, our shadows softly blend,
A sisterly bond that holds, will not amend.
Through whispered secrets and shared, silent sighs,
An unspun silk of memories that ties.

Joy and sorrow in equal measure shared,
Our sisterly shadows, always paired.
Two silhouettes against life's varied hues,
A testament to times we did amuse.

In laughter's echo, our semblance does play,
The shared yesterdays that color our today.
In tangled dreams, our shadow's touch is sought,
Sisterly compass where truth is taught.

The light may shift, yet shadows stay true,
Sisterly bonds in life's grand review.
Through every storm, our shared strength endures,
A force united, timeless and pure.

A Queen's Quietude

In halls of stone where whispers dwell,
A queen's quietude, her pensive spell.
Crowned with duty, a lonely reign,
Her silent thoughts are not in vain.

Beneath her crown, a mind alight,
With strategies born from quiet night.
Each move is painted with a gentle hand,
A soft-spoken force that guards the land.

In the stillness, her heart's resolve,
Through silent hours, her plans evolve.
A chessboard's quietude her best consort,
Her solitude, a regal fort.

Though alone with weight of crown,
Her quiet strength will not back down.
In whispered winds, her legacy's made,
A queen's quietude, never to fade.

Portrait of the Protectors

In the shadowed forge of might,
Where flames dance with glowing light,
Hammer strikes with thunder's roar,
Shields and swords are born for war.

Stalwart guardians of the land,
Keepers of peace with iron hand,
In their eyes, the fires of faith,
Protectors strong against the wraith.

Clad in armor, hearts so bold,
Tales of valor, sung and told,
Standing firm against the tide,
Behind them, safety does abide.

Each a castle, each a stone,
In the wall, they stand alone,
Yet together, they engage,
Portrait of protectors, age to age.

The Shroud of Sibyls

Whispers drift on sacred breath,
Echoes of the oracle's depth,
Tales woven in a shroud divine,
Sibyls speak in cryptic line.

Through the mists of ancient gloom,
Visions from the loom of doom,
They see where mortal eyes go blind,
In the fabric of fate entwined.

Seers draped in mystery's guise,
Weaving truth through prophesied lies,
Their chants, a river flowing wide,
Where past and future coincide.

Threads that twist through time's expanse,
Guided by a knowing glance,
Sibyls bind the ever and never,
Their shroud, the world's truest endeavor.

Chanting with Charmers

Under the moon's enchanting glow,
Chanters with their charms doth show,
Melodies that twist and twine,
Spells sung in a voice divine.

Around the flame they circle tight,
Voices raised through the cloak of night,
Songs of power in the air,
Incantations of a flair so rare.

Harmonies that weave and wind,
Summoning what's left behind,
Charmers chant with mystic breath,
Conjuring life, foreswearing death.

By the power of words intoned,
By the sacred seeds they've sown,
Chanting with a charm so bright,
Cloaked in the full moon's night.

Byzantine Beauties' Ballad

In the heart of a city of gold,
Byzantine stories are told,
Of beauty laced in power's hold,
And secrets that are centuries old.

Beauties in mosaics bright,
Ballads sung in the filtered light,
Of a time when art was might,
And colors fought the endless night.

Eyes that have seen empires fall,
Lips that have kissed the basilica's wall,
The beauties' dance, a timeless call,
In the great Byzantine hall.

Majesty within their gaze,
Their ballad, an eternal maze,
Through whispers of the ancient days,
Byzantine beauties forever blaze.

Petal and Poise

In the morning's gentle glow,
Petals wake from slumber slow,
Symphony of colors wide,
Nature's quiet, graceful pride.

Velvet touch of morning's grace,
Poise that time cannot erase,
Each fold a story to unfold,
In the garden, tranquil and bold.

Whispering to the blushing dawn,
Life in tender hues is drawn,
Soft embrace of daylight's kiss,
Blooms conspire in silent bliss.

In the dance of light and air,
Petal and poise beyond compare,
Nature's art so finely spun,
Until the close of day is done.

Vespers of Venus

When twilight weaves its starry shroud,
And day to night makes solemn vows,
The vespers of Venus shimmer proud,
In cosmic ballet, she takes her bows.

Her gentle light in heavens traced,
A beacon midst the twilight space,
A lustrous gem that night embraced,
Reflecting beauty, time, and grace.

Across the sky, she paves her arc,
A whispered prayer before the dark,
Her presence there to hearts remark,
A celestial flame, a heavenly spark.

In dusky silence, she does inspire,
Those gazing up with fond desire,
To find in stars what dreams may fire,
The vespers of Venus, night's choir.

Captains of Calypso

Upon the waves of oceans deep,
The captains of Calypso keep,
Their steady course, their spirits high,
Underneath the vast, blue sky.

Eyes on horizon, where dreams are born,
Through fearsome gales, their sails are torn,
With hands of leather, hearts so valiant,
They chase the sun, so radiant, gallant.

Tales of glory, seas uncharted,
From loved ones long ago departed,
The captains bold, with courage laced,
On rolling decks, their fates embraced.

Hark the mermaids' distant call,
Beyond the deep, where shadows fall,
Calypso's children, brine and bravo,
Masters of the wind and wave's furrow.

Descendants of Dione

Amongst Saturn's rings they lie,
Descendants of Dione, beneath the sky,
Adrift in silence, in stardust seas,
With the universe as their canvas, ease.

Enigmas wrapped in ice and stone,
Their origins in darkness, largely unknown,
A dance of gravity they gracefully trace,
With time and space at an eternal pace.

In the vastness, they abide serene,
Specters of what has never been seen,
Whispering the secrets of cosmic lore,
Held in their orbits, forevermore.

Children of a distant sphere,
In Saturn's embrace, they persevere,
Descendants of Dione, in motion weaved,
Part of the cosmos they've silently cleaved.

A Diary of Dahlias

In gardens wearing morning's hue,
A dahlia's diary, petals new,
Beneath a sky of softest blue,
Their blooms unfurl as day ensues.

Whispered secrets in colors bright,
Nature's spectrum in sheer delight,
Crimson, purple, a painter's white,
Each page a dance in soft sunlight.

A fragrant breeze, they sway in tune,
Their leaves a cradle for the moon,
Sunset's glow, a serenade's croon,
In dusk's embrace, they softly swoon.

Dahlias' tales in twilight spun,
Scripts of petals, day is done,
A final bow to the sinking sun,
The flowers' diary rests, its song sung.

Gypsies' Gala

Underneath the canvas stars,
Gypsies' gala, near and far,
Twirling skirts and strumming guitars,
Each melody a memoir's memoir.

Around the fire's warming heart,
They dance where shadows merge and part,
Wild spirits, free, they spin and dart,
Life's mosaic, a living art.

Eyes alight with untold tales,
Adventures sail on phantom gales,
The night alive as laughter prevails,
In every cheer, life’s essence hails.

Beneath the moon, their songs ascend,
Joyous notes in twilight blend,
Till dawn's first light, moments they lend,
To the gypsies' gala that never ends.

In the Realm of the Roseate

Whispering soft the roseate glow,
Delicate whispers, sweet and slow,
In petals' poise, the secrets flow,
Within the realm where roselings grow.

Tinged with blush of first love’s dream,
In dawn's young light, a tender beam,
Their fragrance fills the morning stream,
Entwined in life's resplendent theme.

Roseate hues, a tender graze,
Within this garden's blushing maze,
Each stem and thorn, a heart's appraise,
In their world, the sun's soft rays.

Softly they speak, in gentle tones,
A symphony of sighs and moans,
From dew-kissed buds to blossoms blown,
The realm of roseate quietly thrives, unknown.

Odes to the Olive Branch

Odes to the olive branch we bring,
A symbol pure, on dove's light wing,
In placid strength, its leaves do cling,
Harbinger of peace it does sing.

Through ancient groves, in whispers told,
A legacy of fruit like gold,
By Grecian suns and earth enfold,
In olive’s story, hope is rolled.

Noble boughs in reverence sway,
Their silvered leaves a silent fray,
Against the winds of disarray,
They stand unyielding, come what may.

A testament to enduring peace,
As wars may rage and conflicts cease,
The olive branch speaks soft release,
Its odes of harmony never decrease.

Matriarchal Melodies

Guardian of the lineage, strength unfurled,
Her wisdom like a beacon, lighting worlds.
With each tale and tender melody,
She weaves the tapestry of family.

Through time's relentless march, she stands so bold,
In her eyes, the fire of ages told.
Her laughter, a symphony of joy and might,
Echoes through the corridors of night.

Matriarchal melodies, soft and clear,
Resonating far and drawing near.
Guiding through the struggles, through the pain,
A song of triumph, blooming in the rain.

In her embrace, a fortress made of care,
A legacy of love beyond compare.
In every verse, her spirit's dance and swell,
The matriarch's the story that we tell.

Vintage Vignettes

Whispers of the past in objects old,
Stories in the silver and the gold.
Each artifact a chapter from days yon,
In vintage vignettes, life's portrait drawn.

The rustling silk of a gown once worn,
At dances where young love was sworn.
Faded letters holding secrets tight,
Words that set a thousand dreams alight.

Within these walls, the echoed mirth,
Of generations round the hearth.
With every cherished antiquity,
We clutch the heart of history.

Time's golden threads weave memories sweet,
Where sepia tones and present meet.
In every scratch, a moment's glance,
Vintage vignettes' enduring dance.

Lioness Lullabies

In the golden grass, 'neath the setting sun,
A lioness to her cubs whispers, ‘Rest, my little one.’
Her gentle hum vibrates through the savanna air,
Lioness lullabies, a tender prayer.

With a voice that carries through the night,
She serenades the stars that softly light.
Her warm embrace, a shield from fear,
The quiet strength of love draws near.

Echoing through the fields, her mindful song,
Teaching cubs that they are brave and strong.
A purring rhythm, the comfort of her might,
Soothes the wild heartbeat into the night.

Her melodies, a guiding force so true,
Instill the virtues her cubs will pursue.
In every note, a wisdom to abide,
Lioness lullabies, their mother's pride.

Paternal Petals

Through the garden of life, a father's hand,
Guides the growth in the fertile land.
With every seed he sows with gentle care,
Paternal petals bloom forth fair.

His words, like water, nourish young minds,
In the wisdom he shares, the truth one finds.
A steady sun that warms the day,
His love, the light that shows the way.

With weathered hands, he tends each sprout,
Through storms within and fears without.
His silent sacrifices known to few,
The strength in each petal, a hopeful hue.

A bouquet of moments, tenderly held,
The fragrance of his efforts seldom tell.
In every blossom, his spirit we see,
Paternal petals of legacy.

Reflections in Ruby

In depths where scarlet gems abide,
Beneath the earth’s rich, somber loom,
I see myself in rubies' tide,
Each facet casts a different gloom.

In mirrors of the ruby's face,
I find my thoughts in rich, red spill,
Their edges sharp as love's embrace,
Reflecting whispers of my will.

The crimson glow holds dreams at bay,
A dancing flame in shadow's nest,
Creating twilight in the day,
In rubies' fire, my soul's undressed.

My heart, it beats in ruby's rhyme,
While time itself bends to its chime.

Bonds Beyond Bloom

When petals wither, colors fade,
And stems do bow in life's parade,
Remember still the bonds we've made,
Beyond the bloom, our love stays staid.

In gardens where once flowers swayed,
Now silent, lies our shared arcade,
Yet strong, the ties of friendship stayed,
Roots deep as ever, unafraid.

For bonds of love are not just frayed
By winter's touch or summer's blade,
They're in the earth that we have laid,
The memories that never trade.

So even as the blossoms fade,
Our spirits mingled, love relayed,
No distance makes our closeness jade,
In every season, love's conveyed.

Athena’s Aria

From wisdom's throne, the owl takes flight,
Through olive groves in soft moonlight,
Athena's song soars through the night,
Her aria, a pure delight.

In notes of courage, fierce and bright,
A song of war and thoughtful might,
It echoes through the keenest height,
An anthem of an ancient rite.

Through marble halls, and cities tight,
The wisdom of her voice takes flight,
Bestowing insight with her light,
A gift for minds that seek her sight.

In every struggle, in each fight,
Remember her melodious right,
The goddess cloaked in starry night,
Her aria, a kindled light.

The Summoning of Sisters

Amidst the whispering of trees,
A coven's call rides on the breeze,
Sisters gathered with such ease,
A summoning of souls to seize.

Their circle drawn, a soft appease,
Beneath the moon, they bend their knees,
In unity, their spirits tease
The arcane arts they aim to please.

The air is thick, the veil does crease,
Beyond this world their chants release,
The boundaries of realms decrease,
Reflecting powers they increase.

A tapestry of fate they weave,
With threads of time that interleave,
The sisters' will, they won't deceive,
In sorcery, they all believe.

Printed in the USA
CPSIA information can be obtained
at www.ICGtesting.com
LVHW021638161123
764105LV00005B/119

9 789916 391518